The Phoenix Living Poets

THE OLD ADAM

The Phoenix Living Poets

THE OLD ADAM

by

D. J. ENRIGHT

CHATTO AND WINDUS

THE HOGARTH PRESS

1965

Published by
Chatto and Windus Ltd
with The Hogarth Press Ltd
42 William IV Street
London WC2

★

Clarke, Irwin and Co Ltd
Toronto

Printed in Great Britain by
T. H. Brickell and Son Ltd
The Blackmore Press, Gillingham, Dorset

Contents

Contents

Acknowledgements are due to the editors of the following periodicals, in which some of these poems first appeared: *The Critical Quarterly, Encounter, Granta, The London Magazine, Meanjin Quarterly, New Statesman, Observer, The Spectator, The Times Literary Supplement, The Twentieth Century, Westerly*.

I

THE OLD ADAM

Visiting

Mixing briefly with some
Who've lived for months, years, ages,
Deep down in the abyss,
On lower ledges,

He finds them easy,
Understanding, even almost gay.
How can this be?
He feels the ground slipping away
From under his feet.

So likeable, so considerate,
Yes, even almost healthy
(All their suicides unsuccessful).
How on earth can this be?

Unless they're visitors from above,
From the gayer, easier flatland?
And he the old dweller in abysses
– Apprehensive, prudent, pained –
On one of the upper ledges?

Well, that would explain
The odd resentment they arouse
In him. And the faint ancient pain
Of drawing breath. And his ragged nails.

Labour Saving

Dame Insecurity –
She is our muse,
And in her fashion
The old dear's faithful.

As years grow longer
Lines grow shorter.
Yet, she tells us,
She won't desert us.

She's slipping, though.
– Credit at the bank,
Job seemingly safe
For another month,

Unmentionables
('Can't count on that,'
She says, 'at your age')
In retirement

(Insolent hag!),
The house accoutred
With a shining score
Of lightning conductors,

And a friendly copper
At the corner . . .
Dear me! How to keep us
On our toes?

So, she says,
To save herself the labour
She's found a regular:
Insecurity's big brother –

Death.
The bouncer in person.
Short lines, perhaps,
But hard.

The silly bitch!
Little she guesses
What rods she lays in pickle
For herself. (And us.)

Sailor Ashore

Anchored firmly to her body, now he knows
The crash of rigging, burst seams and sudden flood;
Who hitherto, loose prey of all the elements,
Was blasted by a breeze, wrecked in an inch of mud.

Facing Facts

Velleities and doubts have occupied
    A week.
The pleasing and reposeful role of those
    Who speak

Wisely of what they'll never lie awake
    Because of.
'Maybe he . . .' 'She ought . . .' 'One certainty, it's . . .'
    Not our love.

When all is said and said again, we then
    Locate some pride
In facing facts – that this was all escape –
    And there we hide.

Rhyming

Hunting through reason for a rhyme to paradisiac,
His nose soon leads him to his quarry, aphrodisiac.
Twin instances indeed of short-term fabrication.
He has no need, he smiles, for either titivation.
Non-starters hardly know that impulse, Dionysiac
And vulpine, fair or foul, to further exploration.

The Muse Drops By

At last a visit –
How you begrudge your company!

You were busy, as I knew.
But did you miss it?

Yes, I was busy.
But yes, I missed you.

I missed you too.
But here I am again. Or nearly.

Say something to me then,
Not these vain pleasantries,
Something helpful, something wise.

Wise for what – where – when?
In heroic couplets, or some other metre?
I'm hardly through the door as yet. . . .

Why ask? Me you know much better
Than ever I'll know you . . .

And all the same you keep me
Standing at the door, as if taboo,
In draught and dust?

My poverty
You know too well already!
I won't display it to you.

So faint your trust?
And me so famous and so asked-for, too . . .

How can the fugitive trust the deathless?
My metre ticks too fast.
You pause to draw a breath,
The deadline's past.
So, I am busy . . .

And I respect your busyness.
Believe me, I admire such healthiness.

Were my business only yours!
But you, with all of time,
Can knock at all the doors
In town, find them locked, never mind.
You don't know what waste is.

While you, alas, waste more
To hide your wastage –

Now comes your wisdom, now you'll show
How kind –

While, I was saying, you waste more
On folk you scarcely know,
Gossiping at your door!
I'll go . . .

Come in, please. Do!

I'm halfway down the street already,
You've shamed me into being busy too.

Postcard from Hamburg

In the Musikhalle
Yogis demonstrate stomach exercises
In sundry poses.
In the Reeperbahn
Ladies demonstrate bust exercises
In several phases.
In the Planten un Blomen
Plants and blooms demonstrate neck exercises
In various breezes.

In the Catalogue

It was a foreign horror.
A cold and lonely hour,
A place waste and littered,
And this figure standing there.

Like at first a prized
Cherry sapling swathed in straw.
It was no tree. It was enclosed
In a straw cocoon, and

Wore a hood of sacking
Over the might-be head
And the should-be shoulders.
It seemed to be looking.

What did I fear the most?
To ignore and bustle past?
To acknowledge and perhaps
Find out what best was lost?

It didn't accost. I did.
Rattling in my outstretched hand,
I hoped that money would talk,
A language of the land.

Some inner motion stirred the straw.
My stomach turned, I waited
For its – what? – its rustling claw
Or something I could not conceive.

What happened was the worst.
Nothing. Or simply, the straw
Subsided. 'Please, please!'
I begged. But nothing more.

Fear is glad to turn to anger.
I threw the money down and left,
Heedless of any danger,
Aside from vomiting.

From twenty yards I turned
To look. The shape stood still.
Another ten yards, and I strained
My eyes on icy shadows –

The shape was scrabbling for my coins!
I thanked my stomach. Then
Thanked God, who'd left the thing
Enough to make a man.

Flesh and Blood

From early days I dreamt of you,
And woke up choking.
Your unnatural nature, waking,
Deranges me more abjectly.
Sense flies out when you fly in.

Now here you lie,
Your shabby cloak, torn open, shows
Blood in a meagre ooze
(Plainly, so poor, your own)
And a rich clutch of fleas –

Your own, yes, all your own,
Even your own face.
No teacher's out of early days,
Or later woman, headline, bellyache
Or ache of mind.

And so your natural death
Absolves your dubious nature.
Your brotherhood no longer
Shall play cat and mouse with me!
– But see, sense takes to flight again,

My dreams still flap their wings,
They say, they are no dream:
As monstrous cats afflict
The dreams and waking of your kin,
A cat caught you at last, in fact.

Laws

Having broken some
Of the laws of God,
And more of man,

What now remains
To frame or fill
The remnant of a life?

Severity is out,
The patent probity
That wins promotions,

And thrift belongs
To good wives, good mothers,
To the good,

Likewise the assurance
That sad stories
Are only stories,

And rest –
None, as we know,
Of this for the wicked,

And so I see her
(With such respect
For all those laws)

Here, there, everywhere,
Tireless with cash
And kindnesses,

Consumed by
Cruel and radiant fires –
A woman once bad,

Doing through the long
Remainder of a life,
Exactly, good.

Weak Characters

Now that my tale is told and posted,
I leave the rest to silence and to you.
There's room, God knows, for some improvement.
I left your souls at bottom to yourselves,
And fifty years or more for you to fill,
Barring accidents, just as you will, and
Neither's prone to accident. Credit I take
Or otherwise for a mere month or so
Of actual living, and the bare bones
Of your formal schooling. Man and wife
I made you, as seemed fit and proper;
And made you see the wisdom of my choice.
I have implied – only that, and nicely –
The possibility of family
Not less than nine months after laying down
My pen. I like to think I've done for you
Neither too much nor yet too little.
Regard yourselves. I've handicapped you with

The minimum of ills – a tendency
To hiccups, or scholarly allusion –
And endowed you with no mean advantages,
Better health than mine and nicer natures.
Yet, hand in uneasy hand, you linger,
Unable to repair to work or bed
Without my blessing, or dictation.
So pale you are – when was it you last ate? –
And so reproachful, who should be so pleased.
Friends, we were never more than friends, good friends,
And now our paths divide. The loss is mine.
Move on, you're not my pensioners, move on!
Show your defiance by some novel act,
Take up smoking, or turn Catholic.
My hands are too much inked with you already,
Go in peace or go in war, but go!
Write some new chapter – destitution or
Divorce or death – but not for me to read.

Viewing a Japanese Master

What ordered power! Such colours
And such forms! A molten swirl
As if of robes of ancient days,
Soft pastels and stern primaries,
A line which bears you where it will.
The master at his most assured,
Not one hair out of place.

Only the policeman's eye
Could turn this flux to stone:
And find a monstrous weapon there
Rooting in a melting wound,
Robes which swirl so not to hide
A detailed satyr on a staring girl,
And every hair in place.

The law of paint is ours,
Which feels no itch nor scratch.
Split tree or girl's not our concern,
The taster does not drink the wine.
Line, shape and colour fill their whole,
They bear us where they will,
Not one hair out of place.

Works Order

First and foremost and forever
Remember:
A poem is a work of art
Is a poem.

Do not stray far from the village pump:
Once you have strained your roots
They will never be the same again.
Stay close to the village pump,
You can wash your hands at it
Whenever called for.
In your periods of composition
Close tight the door and windows
And keep them tightly closed throughout.
See that you yourself stay tight throughout.
Pardon me?
Your composition should be tight,
Screwed right to the hilt.
Never use two words
Where one would be meaningless.
Remember:
Understatement has the advantage
Of immunity to contestation.
There are concerns and concerns,
Be careful which you concern yourself with.
The well of English must not be defiled.
As a day-to-day velleity
Humanism has much to recommend it,
But we hardly want it hanging around
In a poem.
Do not make that old mistake,
Confusing art with allegory.

For a poem is a work of art
Is a poem.
Life is short, art has no end.

The Rules

Away from the dream's hard fist
He turns and twists his flesh:
A moment's shelter, then
The bedsprings sound the bell.

He lasts another round.
This dream seems made of stone,
A shapeless cloud of stone.
At last time's up, he turns away.

Until the bedsprings sound the bell.
Why can't some pressing message come
To call him out of this small ring?
That dream seems bigger every round.

Why don't you stop it, referee –
You see that I'm out-weighed, I'm out?
In the name of conscience I cannot:
The answer comes: and that's my name.

Dream! he cries: here is our common cross,
You sweat, I bleed, to make his sinecure!
Where? grunts that dark and stony fist:
There's only you and me, you made the rules.

Silences

The silences that lie
Between the poems,
The silences that lie
Elsewhere –

Heart lying open
(Not policy, not policy,
But accident),
Heart's ears open

To the silences that lie
Between
And seem a sort of lie
But still may be a part of truth

(Truth being what it is,
Not wholly sweet,
Not lying quite too deep
For taint),

Things said;
And followed by a silence,
Not followed up –
Meaningless statements?

I no longer know
What meaning is,
Such silences lie,
They lie between.

Poet Wondering What He is Up To

– A sort of extra hunger,
Less easy to assuage than some
– Or else an extra ear

Listening for a telephone,
Which might or might not ring
In a distant room

– Or else a fear of ghosts
And fear lest ghosts might not appear,
Double superstition, double fear

– To miss and miss and miss,
And then to have, and still to know
That you must miss and miss anew

– It almost sounds like love,
Love in an early stage,
The thing you're talking of

– (but Beauty – no,
Problems of Leisure – no,
Maturity – hardly so)

– And this? Just metaphors
Describing metaphors describing – what?
The eccentric circle of your years.

2

THE CREATURE'S NATURE

Alexandrian

The free minds
Tell us freely about their freedom.
I myself prefer
To face the fact of my unfreedom,
And to speak from that.

I have signed round robins.
Protests against Caesar,
Protests against Brutus,
Protests against Octavius.
I can say I have protested.

And will continue. Habit dies hard.
But I know the truth of my unfreedom,
And know that I myself am not
An overwhelming argument for free survival.
But I do know those who are,
A few who are,
Without reproach or reservation.
Which gives my speech a sentimental tinge –

Sans principle, in open country,
All my shelter is this drooping shield.

Prime Minister

Slowly he ticks off their names
On the long list:
All the young political men.

As he was once himself.
He thinks of how he despised the others
   – the a-political,
      the English-educated,
         the students he called 'white ants
In their ivory tower.'

Not so long ago, in fact,
He coined that happy phrase 'white ants'.
How he despised them, all they cared for
Was lectures, essays and a good degree!

A small thing these days
   – he tells himself –
To be arrested.
Incredulously he remembers
Not once was he arrested, somehow.

Slowly he ticks off the names
On the list to be arrested.
Tonight, isn't it? Yes,
Between 2 and 4 when the blood runs slow.
The young political men,
Full of fire, hot-blooded.
     – For a moment,
He thinks he sees his own name there.
'Red ants,' he hisses,
Thrusting the list at a waiting policeman.

Meeting the Minister for Culture

– At a party.
In that borderland between
Apologetics and apology:
Neither wishing to revoke,
Neither wishing to provoke.
While tacitly agreeing
That the weather,
The latest drainage schemes,
The brand-new Parliament House,
Are hardly worthy themes.

> He talks about United Nations,
> A large and distant subject –
> In the accent of the region
> (The accent which recalls
> So many pretty girls);
> One listens to the accent
> Rather than his news
> (The accent will last longer
> Than this particular voice,
> These particular views).

Then I talk about my students,
A cultural matter.
And he prefers the past
(Before he was a Minister),
And I prefer the present
(Since I became Professor).
I can't deny his past,
He can't deny my present.
The ice we skate on
Is more than thick enough.

Then, after all,
He talks of Parliament House,
Its brand-new architecture,
A cultural matter.
Which blends the occidental
(Walls of glass)
With (horn-rimmed roofs) the oriental.
But is curiously ill-lit.
Already two have walked alas
Through its walls unwittingly.

The story takes our fancy.
Teller and listener laugh,
Each in the accent of his country.
I start an explication
Of this transparent allegory –
And then remind myself,
It's no tutorial session –
And fetch beer from the fridge.
Such warmth might melt the ice
On which we skate so nicely.

Government

There is no end to motions,
There is no limit to amendments.
Each word calls up its enemies,
Dancing with tomahawks in your tents.

All, all are dressed in borrowed robes –
No more a cowboy you, than he an Indian.
The abstract enmity alone is real;
And quite lost sight of, bare forked man.

The decks run red with dialectic blood,
In our wash strange creatures flounder.
We experts steer the ship of state,
While all around old friendships founder.

Had he his hurts before, you ask? –
We have our pride. Shamed be whoever cries
'Enough!' – He has his hurts behind as well.
(A nasty sight for ladies' eyes!)

The oak tree crashes in the wind,
Even the reed grows sick with bending.
Lie doggo, like a log, for what
Is down can suffer no descending.

Limbo is where they still enjoy themselves
– Dim lights and music! Innocent and strong,
No motion rocks their brain, and
No amendment furs their friendly tongue.

– There, with pretty ladies in a ring,
Fat with food and drink and smiles,
There lies a log. Or crocodile perhaps.
Ah well, long live such private crocodiles!

Misgiving at Dusk

In the damp unfocused dusk
Mosquitoes are gathering.

Out of a loudspeaker
Comes loud political speaking.
If I could catch the words
I could not tell the party.
If I could tell the party
I would not know the policy.
If I knew the policy
I could not see the meaning.
If I saw the meaning
I would not guess the outcome.

It is all a vituperative humming.
Night falls abruptly hereabouts.
Shaking with lust, the mosquitoes
Stiffen themselves with bloody possets.
I have become their stews.
Mist-encrusted, flowers of jasmine glimmer
On the grass, stars dismissed from office.

Political Meeting

Nothing human is alien to me.
Except knives, and maybe the speeches
Of politicians in flower.

Dampness, of decay and growth,
Arises all round us,
Indigenous mist from earth's two-way flow:

Can you make out which is which?
I could fall down and rot right on the spot,
Equally I could knife this orator

With all the gusto of youthful delinquency.
Except that the knife is alien to me.
One must hold on to some inhibitions –

Though I still feel the haft in my fist.
God help us, he is only talking,
His expression blurred in the general haze.

A knowing man, doing his job,
Quoting nimbly from several literatures,
Joking with his sworn professional enemies.

Laughter coughs through the mist,
Students hoot genially, a child falls
Out of a tree, bulbs and innuendoes crackle,

And solemn pressmen keep the score
(The workers, perhaps, are working).
We all behave in the manner expected of us.

Then am I pedantic, to look for knives
In the hedges and a mist of blood?
We can't make out our friends, we drift off singly.

Change

Times have changed.
Remember the helplessness
Of the serfs,
The inexplicable tyrannies
Of the lords.

But times have changed.
Everything is explained to us
In expert detail.
We trail the logic of our lords
Inch by inch.

The serfs devised religions,
And sad and helpful songs.
Sometimes they ran away,
There was somewhere to run to.
Times have changed.

Making Certain

Perhaps you are not a mosquito.
Your wings are morphologically akin.
Your locomotion is not dissimilar.
Smaller? Yes, but
You could well be immature.
(It would pay you to make your position clear.)
You display that sort of zealous nose,
Those bandy legs.
Also, admittedly, an atypical hesitancy
In confrontation, almost a trustfulness.
Perhaps you are not a mosquito.
We shall never know for certain
Now you are squashed.

Social-Realist

So he composes what he must.
Memos, business letters, all the
Prose that keeps him in his post.

'I would write fiery verses,
Pity for the poor, for the oppressed
A hope, and hatred for the bosses.'

A woman visits him, whom he
(At her suggestion) once seduced,
And weeps a while, half-heartedly.

'For love the whole world cries,
Love is understanding.
My metaphors would dry their eyes.'

Rain falls like silken whips.
He must forgo his evening walk
Along the sea, past waiting ships.

'I would race out, in storm,
To storm the ironclad ministries,
My words cold steel, my body warm.'

The blood runs slow, flesh withers,
Tethered to his bones. 'I'd gladly give
My flesh and blood and bones for others!'

Memorial Service for a Saintly Person

Perhaps, if he's
To rest in peace,
It needs that
Some of these,

For whom he cared
In his short crowded time,
Should live in peace;
With whom he shared

His so short time,
Crowded with war;
That they should know
Something more

Than what they
Shared with him before?
Simpler to say
In this composed

And special place:
Rest in peace –
You're dead and gone,
No damn for these

For whom you cared.
– Our memorial
Is to an old and live
And kicking devil,

Who in his grace
Keeps our composed and
Special lives, and
Saints in their place.

Small Hotel

Not *Guest* –
The Chinese, those corrected souls, all know
A guest is never billed, whereas the
Essence of my aspect is, I pay –

But *Occupier*. Good words cost no more.
The Occupier is hereby kindly warned,
It is forbidden strictly by the Law
– In smudged ungainly letters on his door –
Not to introduce into this room
Prostitutes and gambling, and instruments of
Opium Smoking and spitting on the floor.

By Order, all the lot, *The Management.*
The Chinese have immense respect for Order,
They manage anything you name, except

To keep their voices down. Outside my door
The Management all night obeys the Law,
Gambles and introduces prostitutes,
And spits upon the floor and kicks around
The instruments of opium smoking.

It is forbidden to the Occupier
To sleep, or introduce into his room
Dreams, or the instruments of restoration.
He finds he has his work cut strictly out
To meet the mandates of the Law and Order.

Coffee, frying garlic and a sudden calm
Imply the onset of a working day.
Kings and queens and jacks have all departed,
Mosquitoes nurse their bloody hangovers.

So large a bill of fare, so small the bill!
A yawning boy bears off my lightweight bag,
Sins of omission make my heavier load.
Insulting gringo. Cultural-imperialist.

Maybe a liberal tip will mollify
The Law, the Order, and the Management? –
With what I leave behind on that hard bed:
Years off my life, a century of rage
And envy.

Reminder to a Symbol

To live as martyr,
The saint we all so badly need –
The man must die.
If not the kind of death decreed,
He still must die.

Like for instance Agnes
– Who was meant for raping,
But then her hairs sprang out
And wrapped her in her maidenhead.
– Who was meant for burning,
But inexplicably
The oil-soaked faggots all went out.

But Agnes had to die,
No other possibility.
– Marry and raise a family?
Write copy for 'Your hair restored'
Or fire insurance?

After this endurance
She had to die.
A casual guard pushed in his sword,
With no one there to see,
No inexplicability.

Too many wonders spoil the saint.
Martyrs are both dead and living,
But must be dead.
High time, Sir Figurehead,
You came unstuck
– Else we shall merely say,
    'He has the devil's luck!'

A Liberal Lost

Seeing a lizard
Seize in his jaws
A haphazard moth,

With butcher's stance
Bashing its brainpan
Against the wall,

It was ever your rule
To race to the scene,
Usefully or not.

(More often losing
The lizard his meal, not
Saving the moth.)

Now no longer.
Turning away, you say:
'It is the creature's nature,

He needs his rations.'
And in addition
The sight reminds you

Of that dragon
Watching you with jaws open
(Granted, it is his nature,

He needs his rations),
And – the thing that nettles you –
Jeering at your liberal notions.

Doctor Doctor

It's not the easy life you think, this sanity.
Look –
The streets fall down, and blame you
In cracked voices for expatriate indifference.
The lofty trees
(Which you are ever ready to praise in prose or verse)
Look down their noses.
Is the car stopped? Is it the shadows move?
For twenty minutes you have been talking humanistically
To a stone-deaf whore.
Extending your feet to a baby bootblack
You perceive your shoes have been abducted.
Bar-girls will relieve you of the exact amount.
Do not argue. It is the exact amount.
Including the special extras for special customers
On special nights.
You complain to a fat ice-box, you shake
His icy Chinese hand.
The wrong dialect, the wrong tone, the wrong.
(You think it is easy, all this sanity?
Try it. It will send you mad.)
The street is awash with shadows.
White man, do not run over our shadows!
Roll up that map. The streets have changed their addresses.
A small upright clerk will direct you with detailed
And precise inaccuracy.
Monkeys and children stretch out vague talons.
You say you are a professor?
(Catching, through the narrow slits of flesh,
A glimpse of cheongsam.) Let me tell you,
You look very much like a gangster to me.
On the walls, eastern godlings spew into pewter pots.

You have knocked everybody's drink over:
Everybody is drinking double brandy.
This blue-eyed moderation is cold and hurtful
To sensitive native. You not like native?
For reasons stated in the Book of Tao Tschung Yu,
But not amenable to translation, we
Do not stock that brand of cigarette.
Shadows lash out like fly-swats.
At the edge of the jungle
Crouch the showrooms of the car-dealers,
At the edge of the showrooms
The latest model crouches in the jungle.
Bow to the mad drivers.
Do not complain.
In this world you have no alibi.
You disagreed with history, now history disagrees with you.
'Guilty' – plead this – 'guilty but sane.'
Bar-girls are adoring the grand madmen, the police
Wave them on with quiet but burning pride.
Your nerves are twitching with sanity,
Like an epileptic you throw yourself down on
Clutch and brake and floor.
Look –

To Old Cavafy, From a New Country

'Imperfect? Does anything human escape
That sentence? And after all, we get along.'

But now we have fallen on evil times,
Ours is the age of goody-goodiness.

They are planning to kill the old Adam,
Perhaps at this moment the blade is entering.

And when the old Adam has ceased to live,
What part of us but suffers a death?

The body still walks and talks,
The mind performs its mental movements.

There is no lack of younger generation
To meet the nation's needs. Skills shall abound.

They inherit all we have to offer.
Only the dead Adam is not transmissive.

They will spread their narrowness into space,
The yellow moon their whitewashed suburbs.

He died in our generation, the old Adam.
Are our children ours, who did not know him?

We go to a nearby country, for juke-boxes and
Irony. The natives mutter, 'Dirty old tourists!'

We return, and our children wrinkle their noses.
Were we as they wish, few of them would be here!

Too good for us, the evil times we have fallen on.
Our old age shall be spent in disgrace and museums.

Reflections of a Non-Political Man

Obviously they are enjoying themselves.
And it wouldn't do, as the saying goes,
For us all to be alike.

They disrupt thé traffic from time to time,
And congest the ether.
Repetition bores. Controversy obscures.
Some of us dislike their handling of words,
The mean triumphs and the mere sulks.
There are certainly better ways to live.
But we must keep a sense of proportion:
There are worse ways too – for instance,
The gangsters shooting it out in the streets.

Now we are shooting it out in the streets.
There must be better ways to live, it won't do
For us all to be alike.

Ecology

Stay still one single moment,
The salt mosquitoes settle.
Hence our cults, our way of
Life: who must, for fear of torment,
Kick and kick against the pricks,
Scribble with each hand or meddle,
Rock the rump in imminent take-off,
Shrug our shoulders, juggling chips,
And lift the elbow.

The hand-clap dance of St. Mosquito!
Hence our patterns of behaviour:
Who spend our blood to keep it,
Lay waste our peace to reap it,
Each man his hell-bent saviour.
Our doctors too are active.
Only the perfect repellent
Can make us more attractive.
They pursue this last deterrent.

Elegy in a Country Suburb

To strike that special tone,
Wholly truthful, intimate
And utterly unsparing,

A man communing with himself,
It seems you need to be alone,
Outwardly unhearing –

As might be now,
The streets wiped clean of traffic
By the curfew

(Apart from odd patrolling
Jeeps, which scurry through
This decent district),

The noise of killing
Far away, too distant
To be heard, above this silence

(A young Malay out strolling
– If you insist on instance –
Chopped by a Chinese gang of boys;

A party of Malays
Lopping an old man's Chinese head,
Hot in their need to burn his hut;

The riot squad,
Of some outlandish race,
Guns growing from their shoulders),

Until tomorrow's news,
And subsequent White Papers,
Analysing, blaming, praising,

Too distant to be heard
Above this heavy hush
Of pealing birds and crickets wheezing,

Tones of insects self-communing,
Birds being truthful with themselves,
Intimate and unsparing –

But birds are always chirping,
Insects rattling, always truthful,
Having little call to twist,

Who never entertained large dreams
Or made capacious claims,
Black lists or white lists:

It hardly even seems
The time for self-communing,
Better attend to nature's artists.

The Ancient Anthropologist

Let me tell you how it happened. Once
I had my finger on the pulse,
The pulse of a large and noteworthy people.

This pulse was a pile-driver, a pounder
On golden gates and coffin lids, a grinder
Of organs, a kraken, a jetstream of tears.

Believe me, it was swings and Ferris wheels,
Switchbacks and Ghost Trains and Walls
Of Death, dodgems and multifarious booths.

I dug in my heels, hung on by my nails.
Till 'Hands off!' thundered that great pulse,
Though not so great as not to notice me.

Perhaps it misconceived my fingers pressed
Concupiscently? Or set to twist its wrist?
– Activities that fall outside my field.

That was long ago. Today I'm as you find me.
All my articulations flapping freely,
Free from every prejudice, shaking all over.

Mr Weary's Room

To be a doer, it seems,
Is merely to do harm.

Feed a cast-off kitten –
Another cat to kill my birds.

Save my worms from birds –
And starve my pretty starlings.

Boys break my boughs, they also
Fall from boughs and break their necks.

As well without my help
As with my help.

I once lived in a castle. Oh
So many doors, dear me, and windows!

(Who built the castle? That
Was long before my tenancy.)

So tiring! Every vista noted
A fresh wrong to be righted . . .

But now a strict monogamy,
One room, one door, one window –

And still too large a view.
Crawl into my cupboard shall I?

No, I'll buy a crystal globe
With the future floating in it,

A watertight aquarium
Where fish eats fish,

And I cannot lend a hand.
I'll be a seer merely.

Envoi

Blame me, then,
Not the theme,
Not those who acted it
– Grant the dream

Its due distinction from
The damp and twitching dreamer.
Their feet were less infirm
Than my poor metre,

Or, limping, then they limped
Along a path much harsher
Than any line of print,
And much longer.

I use the simile of dream,
Incorrigibly lettered:
Whereas in fact those folk
To fact were fettered:

Smooth-tongued simile
– As if to say,
Don't blame me, then,
In dreams my people wouldn't play

– The artists' alibi:
Prompt to cast off parent,
Friend or stranger, to disguise
Deficiency of talent.

God gave us skill
In self-excuse,
To palliate those pains
We freely choose.

No doubt our conscience smarts
– Our subjects suffer,
Though, in lungs, ribs, lives –
Unchosen, tougher.

At all events, blame me,
Not those, who never meant
To tire you with the tears
Of crocodiles of print.